MW00813565

Mozart
The Wonder Boy

BY OPAL WHEELER AND SYBIL DEUCHER

Illustrated by MARY GREENWALT

Zeezok™
PUBLISHING

Mozart, The Wonder Boy
Written by Opal Wheeler and Sybil Deucher

MOZART, THE WONDER BOY written by Opal Wheeler and Sybil Deucher and illustrated by Mary Greenwalt. Copyright © 1943 by E.P. Dutton & Co., Inc. Copyright renewed © 1962 by Opal Wheeler. Published by arrangement with Dutton Children's Books, a division of Penguin Young Readers Group, a member of Penguin Group (USA) Inc.

All rights reserved. This book may not be reproduced, stored in a retrieval system, or transmitted in any form or by any means, except for brief quotations in printed reviews, without the prior written consent of Zeezok Publishing.

Reproduction for any use is strictly forbidden.

ISBN 978-0-9746505-3-1
Republished December, 2006
Printed in the United States of America

Zeezok Publishing, LLC
PO Box 1960 • Elyria, OH 44036
info@Zeezok.com • 1-800-749-1681

www.Zeezok.com

Here is a book about the most musical boy that ever lived. Fortunately for us he wrote a great deal of music and this we can hear today even though we can never hear him play it. His music is always lovely and you will surely hear more of it as you grow up. Through his music, Mozart will always be to us a wonder child and a wonder man.

Peter W. Dykema

(from the original 1941 edition)

Authors' Preface for the New Edition

Here, at last, is the new edition of *Mozart, The Wonder Boy*, that you have wanted for such a long time. The first book of *Mozart, The Wonder Boy*, had some delightful music, but you wanted still more, and here it is — thirty-five full pages of Mozart music that you will find at the end of the story. And now what a joyous time you will have as you give yourself a beautiful concert, playing the lovely waltzes, minuets, and sonatas, all of them written by Mozart, the Wonder Boy.

Opal Wheeler and Sybil Deucher

(from the original 1941 edition)

CONTENTS

MUSIC

Chapter One

EARLY DAYS IN SALZBURG

SALZBURG

WHAT A BITTERLY cold night it is in the little town of Salzburg, far away across the ocean. The ground is covered with a fresh blanket of snow.

High on the mountainside the gray stone castle shines cold and silvery in the moonlight. All around, the great forests are deep and still. What queer shadows the tall pine trees make. Under their snow-covered branches the little wood creatures are hiding. How cozy and warm they are, safe from the biting wind.

Down in the valley below, the River Salzach winds through the quaint little Austrian town.

Over the narrow bridges and cobblestone streets the town folk are hurrying. They are happy thinking of their snug little homes and the good warm supper waiting.

Old Hans, the cobbler, bending over his work bench, sighs as he hammers the last nail into the heavy shoe.

"Guten Abend," he calls to his friend Peter, the candlemaker, who stops a moment to chat over the news of the day.

Through the marketplace and on just around the corner comes Leopold Mozart. His strong step seems more eager than usual. He turns down the narrow little street, stamps the snow from his boots and begins to climb. Up three long dark flights of stairs he stumbles.

"Ah, home at last," he cries, pushing open the door.

Nannerl runs to him on tiptoe. "Hush, Father, the little brother is sleeping. Do not wake him."

But Leopold cannot wait. He eagerly gathers up the little soft bundle and looks for a long time at his new son.

"Oh, what shall we call him, what shall we call him, Father?"

"Be patient, Nannerl, for tomorrow you shall know."

Nannerl, whose real name is Marianne, has wanted a little brother for a long time. Leopold and Mother Mozart are very proud as they watch their little son sleeping. At last Nannerl will have a playmate.

Of course every new baby must be christened at once, so early the next morning Father Mozart comes carefully down the long stairs, the wee baby held tightly in his arms.

Out they go into the bitter January day. The wind is blowing fiercely, and sends the snow whirling in their faces. Leopold pulls the blanket closer over the tiny head. Across to the great stone cathedral on the Domplatz he hurries with his precious bundle.

In the great church the people are busy with their prayers and do not even notice the baby being baptized in one corner of the big cathedral.

What a long name he is given. JOHANNES CHRYSOSTOMUS WOLFGANGUS THEOPHILUS MOZART. His parents call him just Wolfgang, or Wolferl.

Day by day the baby grows to be a fair-haired, blue-eyed little boy, whom everyone loves.

It is no wonder that the children are happy, with two kind parents who do everything they can to make their home a cheerful one. There are the pets, too — the cat, a dear little yellow canary and Bimperl, the mischievous puppy. Then there is the faithful cook who is so fond of the children and delights in surprising them with their favorite dishes. Every day is filled with sunshine and merry laughter.

Father Mozart is the court composer. He plays the violin, and sometimes conducts the court orchestra. Leopold would like Wolfgang and Nannerl to love music too.

Almost every day there is a concert at the Mozart home. Father Mozart's friends like to come and bring their flutes, cellos and violins. They all play together and oftentimes they write beautiful music.

Mother Mozart laughs to see little Wolferl beating time to the music with his chubby fists.

"Einz, zwei, drei," he counts, keeping perfect time for such a small boy.

Nannerl is seven now and Father Mozart gives her lessons on the clavier. — The clavier, you know, is a kind of piano and looks like this:

Little Wolfgang loves to watch Nannerl take her lessons. He sits very still listening to the music. When Nannerl has finished, he thinks he will play too.

Stealing softly up to the clavier, he stands on tiptoe and presses down two of the keys. His face beams. They sound beautiful together! He plays two more and squeals with delight that he too can make music.

Father Mozart looks up startled. He cannot believe that this three-year-old child is able to play thirds without any help from anyone.

"Perhaps our little boy has a great gift of music to share with the world. Who knows?" — thought Leopold to himself.

What a hard time they have now keeping little Wolfgang from the clavier. He loves music much more than toys. He likes games, too, but especially when there is music with them. Toys must never be carried from one room to another unless there is a march or a gay song.

After much begging from Wolfgang, Father Mozart starts, half in fun, to teach him the clavier now that the boy is four

years old. He wants to learn to play as well as Nannerl — then what fine times they will have playing duets together.

Never was there such a sweet-tempered little boy, and so patient, too. How quaint he looks sitting at the clavier with his little suit made just like Leopold's and his long fair hair hanging over his high collar. His short fingers strike the keys so exactly.

Father Mozart likes to teach him for he learns quickly — a minuet perfectly in only half an hour!

"Run away now — no more until tomorrow," says Leopold at the end of the lesson.

"Only one more minuet, just one more," he pleads.

"Not today, my son."

At this, the boy prances gaily through the house in search of Nannerl.

Whatever can Wolfgang be doing now? He is covering everything with numbers — the walls, the floor — even the tables and chairs.

How queer that he draws no pictures but for hours amuses himself with sums.

More than anything else Wolfgang likes to compose little pieces of music and Father Mozart writes them all down in a copy book.

Here is his first little minuet. Can you play it?

MINUET IN G
(TRACK 16)

Composed in 1761

Fine

Trio.

Play from beginning to Fine

Think of writing this lovely music when only five years old!

What a bright clear day it is. Everyone is busy, Mother in the kitchen with the cook and Wolfgang perched high on his Father's stool at the big desk. He is thinking so hard he doesn't even hear the bird singing in his cage close by, for he is beginning to write a concerto. You know this is very difficult music to write, even for people who study music a great many years.

He digs the pen deep down into the inkwell and makes notes on the paper before him. There is so much ink on the pen that it bothers him, and with his left hand he brushes it on down the paper.

The door opens suddenly and in comes Leopold and Herr Schachtner, the court trumpeter. The children are very fond of Herr Schachtner. He has long been their good friend and knows many games to play, always with music in them.

"Well, well, Wolferl, what have you been doing here?" asks Leopold picking up the inky paper.

"Oh, Father, I have been writing a concerto for the clavier."

"A concerto, Wolfgang? And how does it go? Let me try it."

Father Mozart goes to the clavier and is surprised to find the music extremely difficult to play.

"I will show you," cries Wolfgang.

He tries to play it but his hands are too small.

"You see, it — it is very difficult and must be practiced slowly and carefully before it can be played."

Leopold is greatly excited when he discovers that the music the boy has written is exceedingly beautiful.

"God be thanked for this great gift you have, my son."

Wolfgang looks up with a merry smile — to him there is no one quite so wonderful as Father Mozart.

"When you are old, Papa, I will put you in a glass case to keep you from all harm. Next to God comes Papa."

Chapter Two

A JOURNEY TO MUNICH

IT IS JUST two weeks before Wolfgang's sixth birthday. Everyone in the Mozart household is busy with last-minute preparations. The longed-for day has arrived.

Leopold is taking Wolfgang and Nannerl on a concert tour, for he realizes that the children have music gifts so rare the world must share them too.

Wolfgang and Nannerl have been working hard at the piano with Father Mozart these many months. They have learned many lovely pieces to play in concerts.

"Perhaps they will be asked to play for noble families — yes, even for kings and queens some day," thought Leopold to himself.

Around the corner comes the coach drawn by strong horses that Father Mozart has hired for the journey.

"Come, children, the coach is here," calls Leopold.

Mother Mozart follows the excited children down the stairs, her arms full of warm wraps and boxes of luncheon, for it is January and it will be a long cold ride to Munich. She tucks them in warmly. With a last farewell to Leopold, who climbs in after the children, Mother Mozart waves them off.

A crack of the driver's whip sends them clattering over the cobblestone square to the road between the sharp mountains — off to Germany to the great city of Munich.

Mother Mozart goes slowly up the stairs. The little yellow canary greets her with a bright song. He will miss the children too. But did not Leopold say to be of good cheer, that they will soon be home again?

Clatter, clatter, clatter, on go the horses over the rough roads. They are having a merry time in the coach listening to each other's funny tales and songs. Father Mozart sings:

"There was a crooked man

And he had a crooked pig,"

Hey, —— dee — dle — deedle,

"They started off to town

In a two-penny gig,"

Hey, —— dee — dle — deedle.

They all sing together on the "deedles."

On and on goes the song of the crooked man, everyone making up verses as they go along. The old driver is much amused and nods his head in time to the music.

"There was a crooked man
And he had a crooked pig,"
Hey,—dee—dle—deedle,
"They started off to town
In a two-penny gig,"
Hey,—dee—dle—deedle.

The hours pass and at last, cold and weary, they rumble into Munich. Out they climb, bundles and boxes and are soon comfortable in their new lodgings.

A few days later Leopold comes hurrying into the room.

"Come quickly, my children. We are to go to the palace at once. You have been invited to play for the great Prince Joseph, and his carriage is waiting now at the door!"

In a short time the children are dressed in their finest costumes and before there is time to think of anything more they are on their way and soon arrive at the court of the prince.

The audience is waiting and anxious to hear these little musicians.

Wolfgang is very serious when he plays at the clavier for he thinks of nothing but the beautiful music.

The nobles of the court stand near the little boy and listen in amazement to this wonder child. Nannerl, too, does her part, sitting very straight beside the little brother as they play delightful duets together.

Shouts of "Bravo!" and ringing cheers greet these little musicians when the concert is ended and many beautiful gifts are presented to them — costly jewels and rare pieces of lace.

Leopold watches with great interest and is happy that his two children have so pleased this noble company.

Three weeks pass quickly filled with many concerts and now the Mozart children are praised in every part of Munich.

They do not like to leave this beautiful city but the time has come for them to return to Salzburg and off they start.

Mother Mozart is glad to see her dear ones home again after their long journey. She cannot hear enough of their exciting adventures and of the great success they have won. "Now you must practice hard so that you will play even better in other cities we shall visit," says Leopold.

Wolfgang likes to surprise Father Mozart with little melodies that he composes, for his mind is full of them and he is always eager to see them written on paper.

One day when he is six years old he composes this Minuet in F.

MINUET IN F
(TRACK 17)

Composed in January, 1762

Isn't it a bright little tune? Aren't you glad that Father Mozart wrote it down for all the world to play?

"A concert, a concert!" cries Wolfgang as he sees some of Father's friends coming into the room carrying their instruments.

Running for his little violin that has just been given him, Wolfgang stands near his friend Herr Schachtner.

Leopold sees the child holding the tiny instrument ready to play, his eyes bright with excitement.

"You must go now, Wolferl," says Leopold, "we are going to try Herr Wentzel's new trios. Now then, Wentzel, you play first violin, Schachtner the second and I will join you."

The stands are put in place and all is ready. But still Wolfgang stays near.

"Off with you, little one. You must not bother us now. You cannot play yet. One must take lessons on the violin to play with others, you know."

At these words the boy weeps bitterly. Herr Schachtner cannot bear to see him so distressed.

"Come, Leopold, let the child play beside me. He cannot possibly be any trouble to us."

"Well then, Wolfgang, you may stay. But you must play so softly no one will hear you."

The little boy smiles happily through his tears and with the others, begins to draw his bow quietly across the strings. As the music goes on, Herr Schachtner plays more and more softly and then stops altogether. Leopold looks surprised to see that Schachtner has put down his bow.

What! The boy playing the part all alone? Leopold cannot believe his eyes.

The music comes to an end.

Wolfgang's playing is greeted with cries of astonishment and Leopold stands with tears in his eyes looking down at the little boy.

How can it be that this child is able without any study to play this difficult music!

Wolfgang amazes them further by trying the even more difficult first violin part.

The three men shake their heads in wonder.

"We must watch the boy carefully," says Herr Schachtner, "he will one day astonish the world."

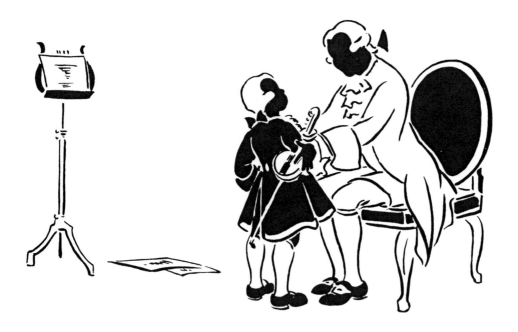

Chapter Three

THEY PLAY FOR THE QUEEN

"WHAT! JOURNEYING AGAIN?" cries Herr Schachtner coming in early one September morning to find Mother Mozart busily packing in the middle of the room.

"Yes, Herr Schachtner, and now we all go together. What fine times we shall have in the gay city of Vienna!"

In rush the children.

"We are going to Vienna, Herr Schachtner, to Vienna! Do come with us," they cry.

The jolly trumpeter shakes his head.

"Perhaps another day I will go with you. Ah, Vienna, how I long to see it."

There is much running up and down stairs with trunks and boxes. Then came the violin and clavier which they strap tightly to the roof of the coach.

At last all is ready.

"Auf Wiedersehen," calls the cook as she waves them a last farewell.

Mother Mozart settles herself in one corner of the carriage with Nannerl beside her. Leopold sits opposite with

Wolfgang, who swings his short little legs and hums a merry tune. He likes to ride in a coach and listen eagerly to the rhythm of the horses' hoofs as they go briskly along.

It is a bright crisp day. The forests are ablaze with autumn colors — deep reds and bright golds shine in the sunlight.

On and on they travel through the beautiful countryside. It grows chilly in the coach when the sun goes down and they pull the carriage robes closer around them.

Slowly the hours pass.

Late that night they arrive at their first stopping place. The children sleep soundly and are anxious to go on the next morning.

Many long days, yes weeks, they spend in weary traveling, but there is always a night's rest at an inn along the way.

Here and there they stop for the children to give concerts and everywhere they are warmly welcomed. But all the praise and beautiful gifts they receive do not spoil these children, you may be sure.

Think of traveling for almost four weeks in a coach over bumpy dirt roads. Often the Mozarts do not have very comfortable beds or tasty food but they are happy just the same.

Day by day they draw nearer to Vienna.

They are delighted one morning to find themselves on a boat sailing down the beautiful River Danube. The children cry out with joy as they pass stately old castles high on the river banks.

When they arrive at the border what a time the Mozarts have at the custom house trying to collect all their belongings. They are wondering what they will do with all the costly presents the children have been given. Their fears do not last very long, for Wolfgang takes out his violin and plays a gay little minuet.

The officials stand about and listen in amazement to the music of this small boy. Custom duties are forgotten and the family is allowed to go on without any more delay — thanks to little Wolfgang.

Everyone in Vienna has been waiting to hear these gifted children, for their fame has spread far and wide.

Finally, in October they arrive in that delightful old city. They are glad to be in comfortable lodgings once more.

Invitations soon come pouring in for them to play for princes, counts, lords and ladies, and now all Vienna talks of nothing but the little musicians.

Leopold has been waiting anxiously from day to day for one special invitation. One morning it comes.

"Good news! Good news!" cries Father Mozart. "The great King Francis the first and Queen Maria Theresa have requested our presence this day at the royal court. Our children are to play for the royal family."

Mother Mozart hurries about, washing and pressing and getting everything ready for this great event.

The children are delighted when they see the gilded royal carriage which has been sent especially for them.

Off they go at a brisk pace to the great castle at Schönbrunn. Soon they are led from one vast room to another until they come to the royal suite.

Leopold and Mother Mozart are filled with awe as they are presented to the king and queen. But not so the children, for Wolfgang likes the queen at once. He runs to her, springs into her lap and kisses her.

Maria Theresa is much pleased, and turning to the Mozart family presents them to the royal children. It is not long before Wolfgang and Nannerl are romping gaily with the princes and princesses.

It comes time for Wolfgang to play. He steps quickly to the clavier, bows very low and begins. The royal family sit motionless, listening to one beautiful solo after another.

Nannerl watches her little brother fondly until it is her turn to play.

Afterward come the duets together and last of all violin and clavier sonatas. What a sweet tone Wolfgang has and how perfectly in tune he plays on his violin. The king and queen are greatly impressed with the little Mozarts.

"Ah, but it is so easy to play with two hands. Now we shall see what you can do with one finger," says King Francis.

But nothing disturbs Wolfgang. He plays just as clearly and easily with one finger.

The king, not yet satisfied, remarks, "Yes, it is quite simple when you can see the keys. Now we shall cover them with a cloth and then see what will happen."

The boy plays as perfectly as though the cloth were not there.

"Bravo! bravo! little man," cries the king, patting him on the shoulder.

Little Wolfgang gets tired of doing these tricks at the clavier. He does not like to trifle with music for he loves it far too deeply.

Many times they are asked to play at the royal castle. King Francis has grown very fond of the little boy and takes his favorite place next to the clavier whenever Wolfgang plays.

One day the little musician asks for Wagenseil, the court composer and music teacher of the royal children. When he arrives Wolfgang points to the king's chair.

"Sit there, please, Herr Wagenseil. I am going to play one of your pieces and I would like to have you turn the pages for me."

While Wagenseil obeys, the king has to find another place to sit and this amuses him highly.

One little princess is about Wolfgang's age. He likes her very much. Her name is Marie Antoinette. They are having a happy time together, chattering away, one little princess on one side of Wolfgang, and Marie Antoinette on the other.

The floors are highly polished and very slippery. Suddenly Wolfgang trips and falls. Little Marie Antoinette bends down quickly and helps him up. He smiles at her.

"Thank you. You are kind. Some day I will marry you."

"But why would you like to do that?" asks the queen, who is standing near.

"Because she was kind and helped me while her sister did nothing at all," answers the little boy quietly.

The royal family have grown to love the two little musicians and now they are the favorites of all the royal court. Beautiful gifts are showered upon them — shining swords, old tapestries, handsome shawls, snuff boxes and jeweled rings.

It is Queen Maria Theresa's birthday. To the Mozart lodgings come two beautiful presents sent by the good queen herself. Two little court costumes that were made for her own royal children.

If you could only see Wolfgang's! It is ivory color with two shining gold borders and it has a little flowered silk waistcoat. Can you see him in this lovely costume with his powdered wig and bright sword?

Nannerl's is of shining white silk and sewn delicately all over it are colored ornaments. They wear these beautiful costumes almost every time they give a concert and look like little royal children indeed.

Wolfgang and Nannerl have to be up late at night giving concerts and many times they are weary.

One day Wolfgang becomes very ill and the doctor is called.

"Hm!" he murmurs, "scarlet fever! No more concerts for you for a long time, my little man."

Everyone is distressed. Mother Mozart gives him the best of care and in four weeks he is up, and again playing at the clavier.

But Wolfgang is quite weak after his long illness and does

not seem to grow strong quickly, so Leopold decides it is best to go home. The packing begins and they are on their way.

The roads are bumpier than ever and in many places they have to make new ones as they go along. The journey seems endless.

At last, in January, they find themselves home once more after four long months away.

What glowing tales they tell their old friend Herr Schachtner whose eyes get bigger and bigger as each story is more wonderful than the last.

"Yes, Herr Schachtner, it was all very fine," says Mother Mozart, "but our good little home is better than any king's palace in all the world."

"And you, Wolfgang," cries Herr Schachtner, swinging the boy high onto his broad shoulders. "What say you?"

Wolfgang makes a drum of Herr Schachtner's head and striking up a gay tune they go marching through the house as happy as can be while the small drummer sings:

"Concerts! Concerts!

Never enough music for

me!"

This is a happy little melody that Wolfgang composes
when he is six. It is an allegro which means quick and lively.
See if you can play it that way:

ALLEGRO
(TRACK 18)

Composed on March 4, 1762

Chapter Four

VISITS TO ROYAL PALACES

WOLFGANG AND NANNERL are very uncomfortable in their tight little court costumes. It is almost too warm a night for a concert, but the good people of Frankfurt are eager to hear the little musicians and Leopold is delighted with the large audience.

The children wait patiently for everyone to be seated, and poke their heads out between the heavy curtains.

"Look, Wolfgang, it's time to begin," cries Nannerl.

All is quiet at last except for the closing of the big doors. With a loud noise they are pulled together and the audience watches closely to get the first glimpse of the tiny musicians.

From the side door come Wolfgang and Nannerl dressed in the royal costumes given them by good Queen Maria Theresa.

How courtly they look! Great clapping of hands greets them as they bow and take their places at the clavier.

"We must not start until all is quiet," whispers Nannerl.

Out of the corner of his eye, Wolfgang sees that everyone is sitting very still and then he stands and announces in a high clear voice the name of their first number. Another burst of applause and the children begin to play.

There is not a sound in the room for all are eager to hear every note of the beautiful music. How smoothly the children play together and with what clear tone!

When the duet is finished the people cry, "Hurrah! Bravo, little musicians! Long live the Mozart children!"

After more solos and duets little Wolfgang comes with his violin. He plays more wonderfully than ever.

The people of Frankfurt are breathless with amazement for they realize that this little boy is indeed rarely gifted. They nod their heads and say to each other, "Indeed he is rightly called a wonder child."

The children forget how warm the night is for they like to play for an audience that sits quietly and listens so well to their music.

Wolfgang's little face becomes flushed, his eyes bright. On and on he plays until after two hours, Leopold announces that the concert must come to a close. The children do not want to stop, for the people call again and again for more music. But Leopold is firm and the Mozarts leave the hall, the applause still ringing in their ears.

"I think I should like to live in Frankfurt. The people are kind. I would like to play for them every night," says Wolfgang in a sleepy voice.

Since leaving home over two months ago they have given many concerts. They liked almost every city. There was Munich where they played again for Prince Joseph.

Then there was Schwetzingen where they heard a great orchestra. Wolfgang was excited as he listened to all the different instruments and sat day after day near the man who played the flute. The two became great friends.

The lovely old city of Heidelberg had been visited too. There to their great joy they found an organ in a church and Wolfgang was given permission to play it. He had played an organ only once before. How little he looked sitting at the great instrument with its tall pipes, but his music filled every corner of the church.

The town folk passing by heard the sounds and crept softly in to see who was playing so beautifully. They were filled with wonder when they saw a small boy sitting high in the organ loft. Wolfgang wanted to play for hours but it was time to go on.

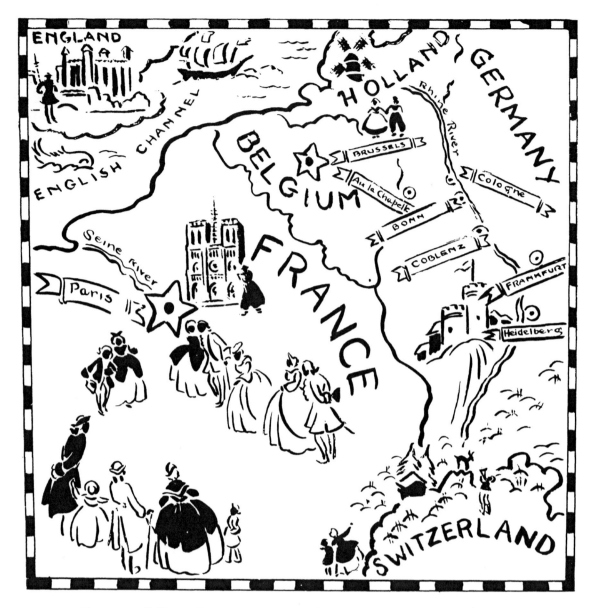

Can you follow their journey on the map? From Frankfurt
they went to Coblenz and Bonn. On rolled the carriage to
Cologne, Aix-la-Chapelle and Brussels.

Where are they going? Why to Paris, the great French

capital. Five long months it has taken them to reach this
beautiful city along the winding River Seine.

They like Paris. It is gay and so different from the other
places they have visited.

Not very far from this city is the king's palace, the court of Versailles. Again the children are to play for royalty, this time for the King and Queen of France.

At the appointed hour they drive to Versailles.

A brilliant sight greets them as they step from their carriage. The great palace is glittering with lights.

As the Mozarts walk through the spacious halls the children are fascinated with the sparkle of the crystal chandeliers. The walls are covered with rare tapestries, the high ceilings gaily decorated with bright paintings.

They pass ladies richly dressed in shimmering silks and taffetas promenading through the long corridors with courtly gentlemen.

King Louis XV and the queen graciously receive the Mozart family. The children play as delightfully as ever. Before the evening is over the king is so impressed he leads the way to the royal chapel where Wolfgang is given the privilege of playing the large gilded organ.

It is long past midnight when the Mozarts are back in their lodgings. They will never forget this wonderful evening at Versailles.

Springtime in Paris! Wolfgang and Nannerl like the long walks with Leopold and Mother Mozart. It is no wonder that the family do not want to leave this happy life, but they have been here for nearly half a year and Leopold is anxious to have the children play in England.

One day early in April they start for London. The children have never seen the sea before and they like to watch the waves beat high against the white cliffs of England.

The British people have heard all about the little musicians from Salzburg and greet them cordially. The concerts in London are even more successful than those in Paris and this pleases Leopold.

As you may well imagine it is not long before they play for the rulers of England. Outside the royal residence the soldiers stand on guard. How tall and straight they are in their bright red jackets with brass buttons.

The children stand watching these serious-faced guards.

"They are like wooden soldiers," they exclaim.

Soon one comes to life and conducts them into the palace.

King George is very fond of music and especially likes the compositions of Handel and Bach. He gives Wolfgang pieces of these masters to play and though the little boy has never seen some of this difficult music, he plays it all without missing a single note.

The king is delighted to have the children come to play for him and he always sits near by and nods his head in time to the music.

The queen's music master is called to hear the children whenever they come to play. His name is Johann Christian Bach and his father, you know, was one of the very greatest composers — Johann Sebastian Bach. Perhaps you play some of his pieces.

Queen Charlotte is kind and motherly and Wolfgang likes to accompany her when she sings.

The children are given costly gifts and toys each time they play at the royal court and at the homes of noblemen.

The Mozarts enjoy walking about London. Today they are sauntering about St. James's Park, throwing crumbs to the hungry birds.

Suddenly Wolfgang shouts, "The king and queen! They are coming this way!"

Indeed it is the royal carriage bearing the good king and queen. They are drawing near and now they recognize the Mozarts.

Down goes the carriage window. King George puts out his head and nods gaily to them as he rides by. Then he waves to Wolfgang who smiles brightly at his good friend.

One day, not long after this, Father Mozart suddenly becomes ill. Mother Mozart is quite worried and calls an English doctor.

"Everything must be kept very quiet in the house so that Mr. Mozart will get well quickly," he tells them.

There must be no noise of practicing, so Wolfgang thinks he will write some music. But what shall it be? A symphony, he decides. Think of it — a symphony at eight years old.

This music is played by an orchestra, you know, and for every instrument you must have a special part to play.

"Come, Nannerl, and sit here close beside me while I write," calls Wolfgang, "and be sure to remind me to give the horns plenty to do."

It is fun for this little boy to write music. When he begins his composition he thinks of nothing else and does not even raise his eyes until he comes to the last measure.

"The symphony is finished," he cries. "I will begin some sonatas next."

Away he goes and in a very little while he finishes not just one sonata, but several of them. He sends them to Queen Charlotte who is so pleased, she sends him a beautiful gift in return.

This melody is a part of one of his sonatas. Doesn't it have a lovely swing?

THEME

From the Sonata in A
(TRACK 19)

Leopold thinks he will get well more quickly if he is in a quieter place than London. So the family moves not very far away to a dear little place called Chelsea. The grass is very green and flowers are blooming everywhere in the great open fields.

The children play out in the bright sunshine all day long, singing and romping in the green meadows.

When Leopold is better they move back into town. Soon they are settled, practicing and giving concerts again.

Wolfgang writes lovely waltzes, too. Perhaps you can play

this one. You will enjoy it, for it sparkles with fun.

A LITTLE WALTZ
(TRACK 20)

"Well, well, another invitation," says Leopold early one morning after moving into town.

"Is it to the king's palace?" ask the children.

"No, this one is from Holland. The Prince of Orange and Princess Caroline have invited us to visit their country. I think we shall go, for one year in England is long enough."

It is very rough crossing the English Channel but they arrive safely. The Dutch people are more than pleased to have the Mozarts come to visit them.

Many times the children play for the Princess Caroline and for the town people, too.

Wolfgang and Nannerl delight everyone with their gracious ways.

After spending many months with these kindly people of Holland the Mozarts go once more to Paris before returning home.

The French people welcome them and are delighted to have them play again.

Never were two children so honored by kings and queens and noblemen at all the great courts of Europe.

And now after this concert tour of more than three long years, they plan the journey home, and on the way, pass through the beautiful land of Switzerland.

"Will this long ride never end," sigh Leopold and Mother Mozart as they peer out of the carriage window eager to catch the first glimpse of the little home in Salzburg.

But all journeys must end some time and with a shout of joy the children tumble out of the carriage and are greeted by the faithful old cook who almost weeps with joy to see her beloved Wolfgang and Nannerl again. How they have both grown!

The children are hurried off to bed for they are very weary. Soon they are fast asleep. Wolfgang dreams of bumpy roads,

horses' hoofs, great palaces, kings and queens, new
swords, bright jewels. Those jewels! They sparkle and
shine so brightly that Wolfgang rubs his eyes and sits up
suddenly.

"Why it's only the sunlight!" he cries. "Wake up, Nannerl,
we are really at home. And listen to our little canary, — he
still sings in the key of G!"

74

Chapter Five

THE WONDER BOY GROWS UP

WOLFGANG SITS AT the clavier in a suit of soft green with delicate pink lining and shining silver buttons. At fourteen, with his bright blue eyes and fair hair, he looks like a young prince indeed.

"Look! It is the ring on his finger. It casts a spell. No boy could play like that," the people in the audience murmur to each other.

The whispering grows so loud it disturbs the boy and he stops playing.

"It is your ring, Wolfgang," explains Leopold. "The people think it casts a magic spell. Give it to me until the concert is over."

The boy takes the ring from his finger and to the amazement of the audience, plays as wonderfully as before. Everyone is spellbound and can hardly believe that so young a musician can have such great power.

Leopold and Wolfgang have been here in the city of Naples for some time. They have visited many other places in Italy, too, for Leopold wants the boy to hear beautiful Italian music.

After the last long concert tour, Wolfgang stayed at home for several years studying and writing music. Each day he spent long hours working with Leopold.

Nannerl is in the little home in Salzburg helping Mother Mozart to keep house. She is always eager for Wolfgang's letters and each day watches anxiously for the post. He writes to her often and wishes that she too might be in Italy, the land of sunshine and song, and especially this colorful city of Naples on the bright blue Mediterranean Sea.

How he loves it all — the concerts by great musicians and the music in the churches. It is here in Naples that many composers are gathered, most of them writing operas.

Wolfgang likes to write operas too, more than anything else, for it is such fun to set a story to music. He also composes church music and many lovely songs. This beautiful one you have probably heard many times. It is called "Wiegenlied" which means cradle song.

It is Easter Week in the old, old city of Rome. Leopold and Wolfgang are enjoying the music played in the churches at this season. They go to the Sistine Chapel for a very solemn service called the "Tenebræ." It is a strict rule that no one excepting

WIEGENLIED

those who take part in it must ever see the music of this service.

Wolfgang hardly notices anything around him in the beautiful chapel with its high arched ceiling decorated by the great Michelangelo. He hears only the music and sits without moving until it is finished. Hurrying home he quickly takes his pen and writes almost every note from memory.

A few days later he goes again to the service, his notes tucked away in his hat. He finds but few corrections to be made.

News of what Wolfgang has done spreads quickly throughout Rome. No one can believe such a thing possible. The boy's music is taken to the chapel and compared with the real copy and to the astonishment of all, every note that the boy has written proves to be exactly the same!

While Wolfgang is here in Rome, a great honor comes to him. He is presented with the Order of the Golden Spur. Leopold is indeed pleased that Wolfgang has been made a member of this high order because of his rare talents.

And now after two happy years with the warm-

hearted people of sunny Italy, they return once more to Salzburg. Mother Mozart and Nannerl are delighted to have them home again. Here they stay for six long years. Wolfgang feels very grown

up in his first position given him by the Archbishop of Salzburg as court organist and concert master. He gives lessons on the clavier, too, and sometimes goes to different cities to write operas at special request.

During all these years Wolfgang never stops composing.

Here is another of his beautiful melodies — a song that is
quite easy to sing:

LONGING FOR SPRING
(TRACK 22)

Come love - ly May with blos - soms And boughs of ten - der green, And

lead me o'er the mead - ows where cow - slips first were seen. For now I long to

wel - come the rad - iant flow-ers of Spring, And thro' the wild - wood wan - der, And

hear the sweet birds sing.

Think of being a great composer at twenty-one, — for that is what people call Wolfgang now. Leopold has given him the finest musical training, but he has been carefully educated in other things as well. Wolfgang has learned several languages and when he visits in other countries, he is able to speak easily with people in their own tongue.

Many years pass and we find Wolfgang living in Vienna where he played for the queen so many years before. His young wife Constance is with him and they have musical gatherings every Sunday morning at their little home.

A visitor whom they are always glad to welcome is the composer Haydn. He is very fond of the Mozarts and thinks Wolfgang is the greatest l i v i n g composer. He is proud to play the quartets that Wolfgang writes especially for him.

One day a young musician comes to play the clavier. His name is Beethoven. He is eager to study, but Wolfgang cannot teach any more pupils. The young man plays and everyone is impressed.

When Beethoven leaves, Wolfgang says to his friends: "Watch that young man. He will make a noise in the world some day."

Wolfgang spends the rest of his short life composing. His days are not always happy ones for they are many times full of care and he has to struggle to make a living.

Just now he is writing an opera and he often works late into the night. He cannot write quickly enough, for melodies come pouring into his mind almost too fast for him to get them down on paper.

Wolfgang is anxious to finish this opera for the people of Prague are waiting eagerly to hear it. They like his last one, called "The Marriage of Figaro," and cannot wait for this new opera to be completed.

The day has been appointed for the first performance. Constance is worried, for the overture which is the beginning of the opera is not yet written.

Tomorrow it is to be given. When will the music be finished?

Late that night Wolfgang begins to write. But he is too sleepy and even the funny stories that Constance tells him do not help to

keep him awake. He cannot sit up any longer and falls sound asleep, the music still unwritten.

When the morning light comes, he is up at his desk and in

just two hours completes the entire overture!

"It is finished, Constance!" he cries, and hurrying down the stairs, the notes still wet on the paper, Wolfgang takes the score to have every part for the instruments copied separately.

Never was so great a work done more quickly — this opera that he names "Don Giovanni."

The theater is crowded and all is ready — the scenery, the singers, in their costumes, and the orchestra. But still Wolfgang does not arrive.

The audience waits almost an hour for the performance to begin and finally the music for the overture is brought in, fresh from the copyist.

Wolfgang enters quickly and takes his place, ready to conduct his opera. Of course the men in the orchestra have never seen the overture until now, but to Wolfgang's delight they play it all, without a mistake.

At the end of the opera the people stand and shout: "Long live Mozart! Long live the master-composer."

After this night, whenever Wolfgang strolls through the streets of Prague, the people everywhere are singing the melodies from his beautiful "Don Giovanni."

In later days comes "The Magic Flute." Some day you may

go to hear this opera. This delightful music is a part of it:

SONG FROM THE MAGIC FLUTE

(TRACK 23)

Wolfgang wrote every kind of music and all of it is filled with beautiful, pure melody. His many great symphonies, sonatas, quartets and operas are giving joy to people the world over.

Some day you may visit the little town of Salzburg far away across the ocean. There you will find the house still standing where lovely minuets and other works that will live forever, were written by Mozart, the wonder boy.

We can never hear enough of Mozart's music. These beautiful pieces that he wrote, you will surely want to play again and again, or listen quietly while someone plays them for you.

SONATINA

A FRENCH MELODY WITH VARIATION

Variation

ANDANTE
(TRACK 26)

RONDO
(TRACK 27)

BAGATELLE
(TRACK 28)

Fine

_p_

_f_

D.C. al Fine

PRESTO
(TRACK 29)

SONATA
(TRACK 30)

MINUET

ANDANTE

PRESTO

ANDANTE
(TRACK 34)

RONDO
(TRACK 35)

ALLEGRETTO

(TRACK 36)

107

SONATA
(TRACK 37)

RONDO

SONATA
(TRACK 39)

112

113

A LITTLE MINUET FOR VIOLIN AND PIANO

(TRACK 40)

LÄNDLER - Secondo

LÄNDLER - Primo
(TRACK 42)

(TRACK 43 is the LÄNDLER - Primo & Secondo Duet)

117

119

MINUETTO - Secondo

Trio

Minuetto da capo

MINUETTO - Primo
(TRACK 45)

Minuetto da capo

(TRACK 46 is the MINUETTO - Primo & Secondo Duet)

COUNTRY DANCE - *Secondo*
(TRACK 47)

COUNTRY DANCE - *Primo*
(TRACK 48)

(TRACK 49 is the COUNTRY DANCE - Primo & Secondo Duet)

COUNTRY DANCE - Secondo
(TRACK 50)

124

Da capo al Fine

COUNTRY DANCE - Primo
(TRACK 51)

(TRACK 52 is the COUNTRY DANCE - Primo & Secondo Duet)

Fine

Meno mosso

Da capo al Fine

Meno mosso

Fine

Da capo al Fine

CPSIA information can be obtained at www.ICGtesting.com
Printed in the USA
BVOW050921220213

313915BV00007B/10/P

9 780974 650531